Meditation
Throughout the Day

By Vasanthi Bhat

First published in 1999 by
Vasanthi Bhat
1196 Lynbrook Way
San Jose, CA 95129

Credits:
Published by: Vasanthi Bhat
Edited by: Rich Slogar
Illustrations: Ranjana Kulkarni
Cover design and book format: Prussia Graphics, Inc.

ISBN# 0-9655499-1-7

Printed in the United States of America by:
Bertelsmann Industry Services, Inc.

***This book is dedicated to
Swami Sivananda***

*With utmost respect and devotion,
this book is humbly dedicated
as an offering of devotion,
at the lotus feet of the great savior
Swami Sivananda,
who shines like a bright star
in the galaxy of the Rishis (sages),
Mahatmas, and Prophets of the world.*

Contents

Acknowledgments

I am forever indebted to God for his constant guidance and blessings that gave me tremendous strength and courage throughout the writing of this book. Likewise, I am grateful to Swami Sivananda for his meditation teachings which helped me to understand my strength and inner power.

A book is never possible without the help and support of many people. In this regard, I am deeply grateful to Professor Srinivas Iyer for sharing his great in-depth knowledge regarding Swami Sivananda and the history of meditation.

My immense thanks to Prussia Graphics, Inc. for designing the book cover and formatting the book.

I express my appreciation from the bottom of my heart to Rich Slogar for his continued support and sacrifice in the editing and writing of this book. Work-

ing with him was a great pleasure as we were able to clarify and express ideas in ways that tremendously helped me express my inner knowledge.

My endless thanks to Ranjana Kulkarni for her dedication and countless hours of sacrifice for illustrating the book within a short period of time.

My respects to Connie Wojton and Bharat Tripathi, Kwik Kopy Printing, Campbell, for assisting me with the scanning and final edit when I needed it most.

My heartfelt thanks to my husband, Mahabaleshwar Bhat, and children, Veena Bhat and Krishna Bhat, for their continued support and encouragement throughout the writing of this book.

About Swami Sivananda

During Swami Sivananda's lifetime, India was undergoing a great transition of political and cultural changes under the domination of two great global forces—the British and the Mohammadans. It was at this time that India woke up from her long slumber under slavery and began the struggle for independence. While Mahatma Gandhi lead the political awakening of India, Swami Sivananda helped lead the religious and spiritual renaissance.

Swami Sivananda started his professional life as a physician, not too unlike many others. He became very successful and continued his practice for 10 years. He gained great experience in understanding the nature of ailments, but discovered that medicine alone could not completely cure the mental, emotional, and physical diseases that afflicted

many people. When he learned the miraculous power of yoga, a sense of great compassion and renunciation came upon him and his life underwent a great spiritual transformation. He spontaneously gave up his medical practice to serve humanity. Like Goutama Buddha, he wanted to help relieve all suffering in the world—suppression, disease, poverty, violence, and old age.

As his first spiritual step, he renounced the world and became a sanyasi and performed the most difficult tapasya (penance). As a result, he awakened and realized the infinite spiritual power (Atma Jnana) which every person possesses.

After this self-discovery and self-realization, he was guided to come out into the world (as Buddha did) and show the path towards divinity for all people, irrespective of their caste, creed, and color.

Throughout India, many people were greatly attracted to the simplicity and effectiveness of Swami Sivananda's teachings. His teachings soon gained eminent prominence. As time passed, his teachings spread all over the world through his disciples (Swami Satchidananda, Swami Chidananda, Swami Vishnudevananda, Swami Satyananda Saraswati, and others).

In spite of arduous spiritual work and guidance, he maintained his robust health up to the last days of his life by strictly and faithfully following what he preached—yoga, meditation, spiritual kirtans (songs), and serving humanity.

Preface

We all wish to achieve something great in our lives. We dream, plan for the future, and struggle to achieve our goals. Whether we are successful and achieve much in life or not, whether we are a celebrity or not even known to the neighbors, whether we are wealthy or poor, it is part of our human nature to experience the full range of human emotions, including depression, guilt, low self-esteem, and feelings of unworthiness.

This booklet is especially written to help people utilize many simple, yet practical meditation techniques to balance their emotions and expand their spirituality. These techniques can help us cope with and overcome difficult emotions while feeling content and even joyful in our lives. Practice any one or a combination of techniques to relieve stress, heal and prevent stress-related ailments, achieve inner peace,

and obtain self-realization (higher consciousness) to respect and love one and all. When you attain the depth of meditation, you can easily expand your potential and begin to realize incredible positive changes in your life.

What I like most in Swami Sivananda's teachings is his utter simplicity and practicality. His simple and practical meditation techniques helped me come out of depression and low self-esteem, without pills or invasive medical treatments. It also helped me unfold my spiritual power.

His teachings contain thought-provoking guidance that can help people of all levels lead a harmonious life. One cannot fail to notice his great love and respect for all religions and great people of the world, such as Jesus Christ, Prophet Mohammed, Goutama Buddha, Patanjali, Swami Vivekananda, Sri Ramakrishna Paramahamsa, Arabindo Gosh,

Paramahansa Yogananda, and others. Along with this love and respect for greatness, he never neglected the underprivileged. He preached love for one and all, irrespective of their condition of ignorance, poverty, disease, or criminality.

As a lifelong student of Swami Sivananda, I offer my humble salutations to all sages, prophets, and enlightened people.

Vasanthi

Introduction to Meditation

"The unbroken flow of thought on any subject is meditation."
Swami Sivananda

Meditation is the practice of mindfulness—living with awareness. The dominant feature of meditation is controlling and focusing the restless and ever-wandering mind. It is extremely important to realize that meditation does not mean creating a blank or empty mind, as some modern teachings suggest. The most effective methods of meditation encourage a positive way of thinking without producing any stress, anxiety, or negative thoughts. Meditation regulates and controls the stream of thoughts and directs it through the proper channels to bring about a harmonious union between the body, mind, and soul.

Ever since the beginning of humanity, many different religions have come into existence at various places throughout the world—China, India, Arabia, Africa, America, and other locations. What is remarkable about the human quest for spirituality over the centuries is that all religions have developed their own kind of meditation as a basis of their practice. For example, Christians call it contemplative prayer; Native Americans call it listening; Japanese call it Zazen; Muslims call it Namaz; and Hindus call it Dhyana. The goal of all these methods of meditation is to reach an exalted state of higher consciousness and inner peace—the common basis of spirituality.

Thus the distinction between most religions is only superficial. As Swami Sivanada said, *"All great religions in the world proclaim the existence of God in the cosmic consciousness as well as in the inner most recess of*

the heart. It is eternal, immortal, and full of bliss. This divinity can be truly realized by the practice of yoga and meditation." Prophet Mohammed self surrendered to Allah through intense meditation and preached unity among people; Jesus Christ spent time alone in contemplative prayer and preached the importance of loving thy neighbor as thyself; Goutama Buddha meditated for a number of years under the Bodi tree to receive the enlightenment to relieve the suffering of humanity.

With the power and universality of meditation in mind, incorporate one or any combination of the techniques shown in this book as part of your daily life. Practice these techniques with discipline and devotion and experience the unfolding of the divine energy (kundalini or chi) to help yourself and humanity.

Beginning the Day

Upon Waking Up

"When you begin your day with balanced emotions, you will notice positive changes and become aware of your hidden powers."
Vasanthi

If you start your day with balanced emotions, you will experience positive outcomes in the day's challenges.

When you wake up and are resting in bed, close your eyes and practice slow breathing while chanting your mantra and praying to God for guidance. Develop a cheerful attitude when confronted with thoughts of the day's challenges and stressful situations. Meditate on the challenges during which you normally fail or make mistakes, and try to remember the positive affirmations you receive. Use them for guidance and support throughout the day.

After Getting Up

"Stretching is a natural tranquilizer."
Richard Hittleman

These simple stretches help improve circulation, relax muscles, strengthen the nerves, and prevent muscle pulls and injuries.

Even after a very good night's sleep, it is natural to notice some muscle stiffness as a result of accumulated tension. Take a few minutes to practice one or more of the standing yoga poses or stretches shown below. If you can, try facing east or north. If convenient, keep a door or window open, or step outside and stretch in the fresh, energizing morning sunlight.

1. Toe stretch   2. Warrior pose   3. Double angle

Taking a Shower

"Refreshing yourself is one of the simple pleasures."
Vasanthi

**Being aware of your body and the time you spend caring
for it is a natural step toward self awareness.**

Cleansing refreshes the pores of the skin and helps energize the body, inviting good thoughts throughout the day.

When refreshing in the morning, try to focus your attention on your body and the sensations you experience. For example, when taking a shower pay attention to the feeling of the water and the cleansing of your skin. You can also use fragrances (natural washing gel, body cream, lotions, or splash) to enhance this activity. Different scents and fragrances have specific effects on your mood. You may want to explore and discover what works best for you.

Prayer

"Prayer helps us commune with God."
Swami Sivananda

Prayer helps develop courage, patience, tolerance,
faith, and the dedication to work hard.

Do your prayer with utmost dedication and concentration. A few minutes of dedicated prayer is better than prolonged prayer without any concentration. Be careful what you ask for. If you are faithful and spiritual, you can get what you ask for. However, to achieve your goals, you must be willing to work hard and make sacrifices, no matter what it takes.

Swami Sivananda said, *"God tests your strength by giving you obstacles in the process of achieving your goals."* Remember to rely on prayer and daily meditation to draw courage, patience, and divine power from within. It is then that you hear an inner voice (divine power) and receive guidance. If you follow the inner voice and guidance, you are sure to be successful in what you do because your divine power will never mislead you!

Asana (Posture)

*"What would one not do for this body, the temple of the soul?
We should so nurse it that it can be put to the fullest use
in the cause of service."*
Mahatma Gandhi

1. **Pose of the moon** 2. **Mountain pose** 3. **Pose of the moon**

This routine helps relieve physical, mental, and emotional tension.

Asanas are postures in which we remain steady and comfortable physically, mentally, and emotionally while breathing consciously.

Asanas help the muscles relax by improving circulation which naturally helps relieve the built-up physical, mental, and emotional tension that can accumulate over time. For example, if you are emotionally disturbed, chest muscles become tight. If you are mentally disturbed, abdominal muscles get tense. If you are mentally and emotionally agitated, your entire body becomes stiff and fatigued.

Practice one or more of the routines* for five to ten minutes to relax tensed areas, relieve tension, and experience a peaceful meditative state leading to contentment, happiness, and spirituality.

---

*For detailed information on the yoga postures, please refer to Vasanthi Bhat's book *"The Power of Conscious Breathing in Hatha Yoga"*.

1. Turtle pose

2. Cat pose

This routine helps energize while relieving physical and mental tension.

3. Preliminary head stand

4. Bowing pose

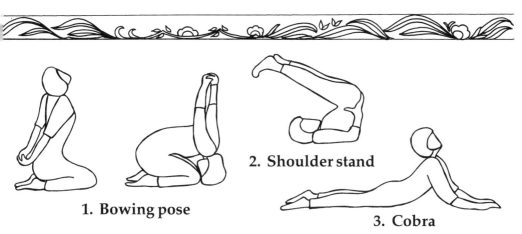

1. Bowing pose

2. Shoulder stand

3. Cobra

This routine releases energy while relieving built-up physical, mental, and emotional tension.

4. Preliminary leg pull

5. Corpse relaxation

Throughout the Day

Faith

"You are a moving temple of God."
Swami Sivananda

Faith helps develop the patience, self-respect, and commitment
that lead to success.

Swami Vivekananda said, *"Every soul is potentially divine."* Believing in ourselves means believing in God. Believing in God helps us develop faith and courage in our life and daily duties. Swami Sivananda said, *"God sees through our eyes, hears through our ears, works through our hands."* With this in mind, we can develop faith in everything we do.

Whether you are a gardener, teacher, executive, social worker, sailor, or homemaker, always remember to believe in yourself and work hard, no matter what it takes. Never compare yourself to others. Then, success and happiness will be waiting for you.

Respecting Others

"Respecting and loving everyone regardless of age, race, religion, and status is spirituality."

Vasanthi

Everyday, try to adopt at least one great quality from others.

Always respect your inner self and follow what your inner voice (faith or intuition) tells you, as long as your actions do not hurt others. Also, remember to respect everyone you come across from all walks of life. Our most precious gift to God is to love and respect everyone.

Everyday take a few moments to get to know the people around you. Everyone has something good to offer and possesses at least a few great qualities. Make an effort to acknowledge and compliment them whenever you notice these qualities. Adopting these qualities in your lifestyle helps you accumulate positive qualities in your life.

Be Kind

"Be kind, for everyone experiences hardships in life."
Vasanthi

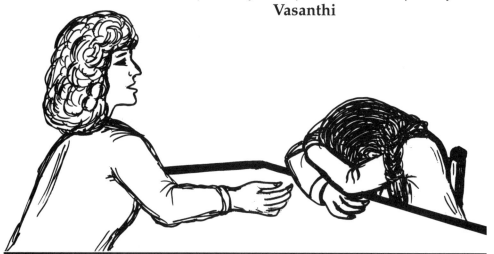

Every act of kindness no matter how small, expands your spirituality.

Be kind to everyone you come across. Regardless of age, status, or situation, try not to underestimate the hardships others face or judge others' happiness.

Everyone experiences hardships at one time or another. Some endure hardships during their early years of life, while others encounter difficulties during the last stages of life.

Ultimately, happiness does not come from status, job, or money. It comes from understanding and caring for others.

Simple Pleasures

"When you are at peace with yourself, everything looks and feels beautiful."
Vasanthi

Simple pleasures soothe the mind and promote inner peace.

Simple pleasures are often appreciated when we are at peace with ourselves. When we are peaceful within, we begin to enjoy and appreciate what we have in life rather than thinking of what we do not have. We also tend to see and appreciate something good in others. This peacefulness helps us be content with what we have.

Take a few moments to thank God while appreciating all the simple, yet wonderful things in life.

Living in the Present

"We are what our thoughts have made us; so take care of what you think."
Swami Vivekananda

Always make an effort to utilize the present positively to brighten the future.

Living in the present moment does not mean we should forget the past or not think about the future. It means we must utilize the experiences of the past to learn, grow, and evolve. Think positively about your future plans while being active in the present.

The present instantly becomes the past. And the future instantly becomes the present. Therefore, what you think right now can modify your past and beautify your future. For example, take a minute now to meditate. Depending on what your thoughts were, your mood will change accordingly. Therefore, take care of the present and the future will take care of itself.

Destiny

"You are the architect of your joy and sorrow."
Swami Sivananda

All your dreams can come true if you have the courage to attempt them and the willpower and patience to pursue them.

Swami Sivananda said, *"Every difficulty is an opportunity to develop your will and to grow strong. Difficulties strengthen your will and turn your mind towards God."*

If your endeavors are pure and sincere, if your motives are genuine and determined, with willpower and hard work (sadhana), you can expect a great success in your work—you can even change your destiny.

Success is not limited to financial and material accomplishments. The most meaningful rewards can come from being content, understanding others, and humbly accepting your roles, such as parent, friend, community member, employee, or other.

Be patient and use any setbacks as opportunities to improve your efforts.

Mealtime

"Eating with balanced mind and emotions improves digestion and nourishes the system."
Vasanthi

A well-balanced meal and relaxed mind are great food for the soul.

Always say a quick prayer and be thankful to God before beginning a meal. This simple act helps relax and calm the mind, emotions, and the entire nervous system. Also, try to focus on pleasant thoughts and conversation while eating. Together with a well-balanced meal, this can uplift your mood and increase your energy.

Resolving Misunderstandings

"When a problem arises, you should be the first to make a genuine effort to take care of it. Don't wait for others to communicate with you."

Vasanthi

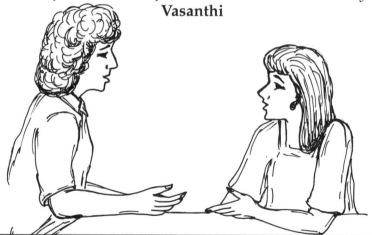

Communicating your true feelings is the best method to get closer to others!

Many relationships end because of misunderstandings or the lack of effort to open up the conversation. When faced with a problem, take a few moments to understand others' situations. Then, try to convey your true feelings tactfully, without hurting or attacking the other person. However, do not always expect others to understand or agree with you. Just sharing your thoughts with others can be a great relief and the first step toward reconciliation!

Mantra Chanting

*"Mantra chanting is like talking
or communicating with a
genuine friend who resides within."*
Vasanthi

Chanting mantra relaxes the entire system and helps you move towards
spirituality and achieve self-realization.

Chanting a mantra is repeating a word or phrase (personal God's name or any other comforting statement) that is special to you. Swami Sivananda said, *"Chant your mantra and commune with God."* Remember to chant mantra as often as possible. Chant your mantra whenever you are depressed, sad, unhappy, agitated, angry, and even whenever you are very happy and relaxed.

Chanting mantra helps us relax the nervous system, balance our energy, and get closer to our soul.

Remember, no matter how much hardship you face, you can always rely on your genuine friend (God) who is always waiting for you with outstretched arms to listen and help you. You can always share your deepest secrets with your inner friend with an open heart, and you are sure to receive comforting consolations.

Karma Yoga

"Performing our duties faithfully without attachment to the outcome is karma yoga."
Bhagavad Gita

Karma yoga helps you perform your duties peacefully and spiritually.

Adopt the principle of karma yoga from the time you get up until you go to bed. Always do the best you can throughout the day, at home, at work, and everywhere you go. Do not worry if the results you desire do not happen as expected.

Swami Sivananda said, *"Do all your work as an offering to God."* This reminds us to perform our duties faithfully while happily accepting the outcomes whatever they may be.

Conscious Breathing

"Conscious breathing is the key to happiness."
Vasanthi

Conscious breathing helps unfold your divine and vital life energy.

When the going gets tough, simply rely on your breath to calm and energize yourself. Whether you are at work, at home, at the gym, in a car, or anywhere else, focus on your natural breath to relieve anxiety and other discomforts.

Always keep in mind that as you breathe, you are also absorbing healing (pranic) and spiritual energy. To your surprise, the answers to your concerns will effortlessly appear, and you will feel more relaxed and peaceful than before.

Driving

"Driving is a good time to be with yourself."
Vasanthi

Driving can be a pleasant break from busy routines.

Make your driving time as pleasurable and comfortable as possible. Listen to your favorite music, appreciate the nature around you, or simply relax your mind by being in the present moment.

When you get frustrated driving, train your mind to think of people who do not have the luxury of owning a vehicle. Conscious breathing will further help you relax and think positively, helping you to appreciate what you have in life.

Anger

"Anger is the #1 killer."
Vasanthi

Conscious breathing helps tame the agitated mind.

When you are about to get angry, pause for a few moments and analyze the unpleasant outcomes of the situation. Expressing anger will only hurt others and make the situation worse. Remember to breathe consciously and contemplate how to deal with the situation without hurting others.

Your breath is a link to your mind and soul. Conscious breathing will help you find soothing answers on how to convert anger into understanding thoughts and caring actions.

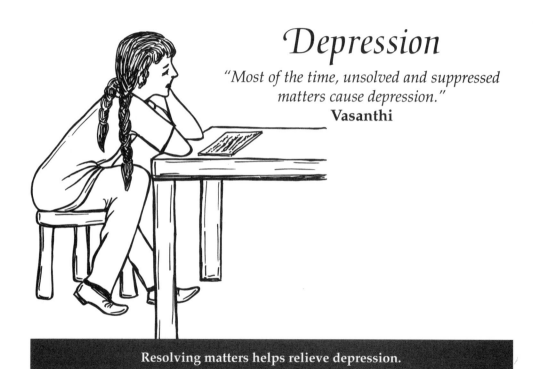

Depression

"Most of the time, unsolved and suppressed matters cause depression."
Vasanthi

Resolving matters helps relieve depression.

"No one is free from pains, troubles, and difficulties," Swami Sivananda said. Everyone experiences occasional mood changes and depression. Some openly express these feelings, while others suppress them throughout their lives.

When you feel depressed, remember to practice vipasana meditation. Understand why you are feeling depressed. It is very important to remind yourself that you are not alone; many others may also be experiencing similar depression. Talk to a trusted friend or colleague and to your surprise, you may find out that your friend is going through (or has gone through) the same or even a more difficult process than you are! Unless it is resolved, depression is like a rocking chair, moving back and forth without going anywhere.

To improve self-esteem, meditate on your accomplishments; to solve difficulties, meditate on how to make the situation better; to draw courage from within, chant mantra as often as you can.

Guilt

"Guilt is a silent killer."
Vasanthi

Forgiving yourself for your mistakes can bring you a new perspective on life.

We can forgive others only if we are willing to forgive ourselves. Swami Sivananda said, *"Mistakes are our best teachers. In the process of evolution, we all make some mistakes."*

Who does not make mistakes or perform misdeeds? Even the great Mahatmas made mistakes. Most importantly, they learned to forgive themselves and were then able to forgive others. When you feel guilty, realize the fallible human condition we all share and try to focus on what lessons can be learned. Promise yourself to act differently in the future and be compassionate with others. This is the first step to self forgiveness and overcoming guilt.

Vipasana

"Vipasana meditation helps purify the suppressed emotions."
Swami Sivananda

Vipasana is a great way to get closer to your soul or inner self.

Whether you are at home, at work, outdoors, or in the midst of a crowd, vipasana meditation is the best method to balance your mind, emotions, and spirit. (If your concentration is good, you can even travel within while keeping your eyes open.)

While breathing consciously, simply travel within. Do not suppress any agitations or disturbances. Instead, try to understand them with a positive attitude. This understanding will help resolve the disturbances by calming your system and guiding you appropriately.

Similarly, when you are extremely happy, practice vipasana meditation to develop compassion for others who are experiencing hardships in their lives.

Ending the Day

Bedtime

"When your mind and emotions are balanced, you are sure to have a restful and refreshing sleep."
Vasanthi

Balancing your emotions prior to sleep is the best way to ensure a comfortable, relaxed sleep.

Prior to going to sleep, take a few moments to reflect on the day's work. If you lived up to your expectations, appreciate yourself and your accomplishments while thanking God.

If you have uncertainties, regrets, unhappy memories, or unfinished duties, you may experience insomnia. Meditate on them while thinking positively or train your mind to take care of them after you wake up by making a list of things for the next day.

Whether you are happy or frustrated, chant mantra to balance your emotions and nervous system to have a restful sleep.

Weekly Meditations

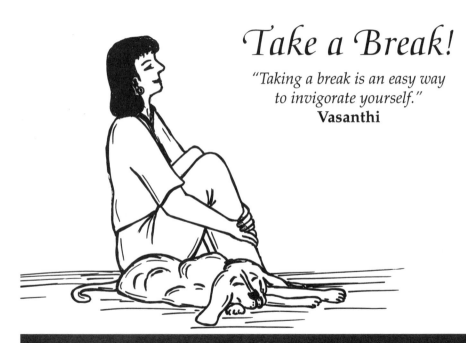

Take a Break!

"Taking a break is an easy way to invigorate yourself."
Vasanthi

Sometimes, doing nothing is simply wonderful.

Every week for at least a few hours, take a complete break from your daily activities and responsibilities. Either do "nothing" or enjoy a favorite hobby or activity where there is no stress or expectations. For example, take a walk, watch a sunset, listen to music, spend time with a friend, or just relax.

It is common to think of doing "nothing" or spending time without a goal as laziness, wasting time, or unproductive effort. Actually, taking a break for a few hours increases your productivity and recharges your brain cells!

Nature Retreat

"Nature promotes peace and tranquility."
Srinivas Iyer

Spending time in nature helps relax the mind and nervous system.

Make a point to appreciate the nature around you. You can go to a park, spend time at a beach, become aware of the flowers and trees in your area, or simply appreciate the changing colors of the sky and clouds.

Getting in touch with nature expands your sense of belonging and spirituality.

Sun Bathing

"The sun is one of the profound sources of vital energy."
Vasanthi

This is a great way to refresh and absorb the sun's natural energy.

During sunrise or sunset, spend a few moments standing or sitting in the sun with your eyes closed while breathing consciously. Feel the warmth and energy bathe your skin and your entire being. Be sure not to spend too much time in the sun or expose yourself to the harsh rays of a very bright sun.

Music

"Music helps us recall suppressed memories and get closer to deeper emotions."

Vasanthi

Music helps purify your emotions.

Apart from listening to music everyday, set aside some time to listen to your favorite music while closing your eyes and relaxing. Music helps open up the suppressed emotions and calm the mind.

This practice naturally helps you breathe slowly and consciously, leading to vipasana meditation.

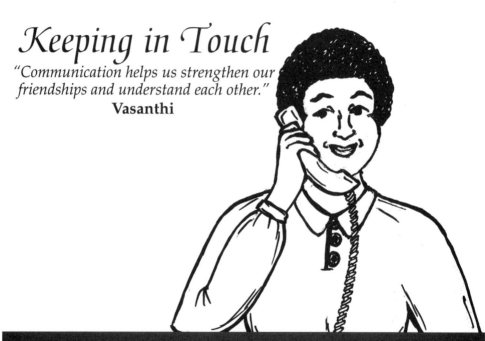

Keeping in Touch

"Communication helps us strengthen our friendships and understand each other."
Vasanthi

Keeping in touch helps others know that you care.

Make an effort to communicate with your friends and relatives that you may not have contacted for a long time. It is very important to keep in touch with the people with whom you feel comfortable.

Regular communication is the best method to get closer to your friends and relatives.

Yearly Meditations

Make Your Home a Vacation Spot

"Vacationing at home gives us the opportunity to explore our neighborhood."
Vasanthi

Home is your paradise on earth.

Often, after taking a vacation we wish we did not go or we need another vacation to recover from the stress and strain of travel.

Take time off from work and transform your home into a timesharing condominium or free hotel.   Act as you would on your regular vacation except explore your local area. With this type of vacation, you can easily save money, avoid the stress of packing and travelling to far away places, and most likely discover some wonderful and exciting things right in your own neighborhood!

This type of vacation meditation helps you appreciate the nature around you. It is not intended to replace regular vacations.

Charity

*"Selfless charity elevates
spirituality."*
Srinivas Iyer

Charity is an integral part of Karma yoga.

Charity meditation is faithfully committing yourself to helping others make their lives better.

Perform some kind of volunteer or charitable work that touches people in a special way. This type of work will help you share what you have and expand your compassion for others.

Vasantha Yoga
Health & Fitness Products

Vasantha Yoga offers a wide range of products for general health and fitness. The video tapes, CD, and books provide a guided yoga practice for people of all age groups and physical conditions.

These products are sold in the United States and Internationally. They offer very clear and simple demonstrations of Vasanthi's unique and gifted style of teaching.

A convenient order form is provided at the end of this section.

Yoga Instructions & Practice Sessions
Beginner/Intermediate
$39.95

Advanced Yoga Sessions
Level I
$29.95

ADVANCED YOGA SESSIONS
LEVEL II
$ 29.95

YOGA FOR BUSY PEOPLE
$ 29.95

YOGA FOR YOUTHS
$ 29.95

YOGA FOR ACTIVE INDIVIDUALS
$ 29.95

YOGA FOR STRESS MANAGEMENT
$ 24.95

PRANAYAMA LEVEL I
$ 19.95

PRANAYAMA LEVEL II & MEDITATION
$ 24.95

YOGA FOR SENIORS
$ 24.95

YOGA FOR SENIORS WITH LUNG AILMENTS $ **19.95**

YOGA FOR THE EYES $ **19.95**

YOGA FOR PREGNANT WOMEN $ 19.95

MEDITATION FOR ALL WALKS OF LIFE
COMPACT DISC
$ 12.95

THE POWER OF CONSCIOUS BREATHING IN HATHA YOGA $ 19.95

Vasantha Yoga Order Form (25% DISCOUNT with the purchase of this book)

VIDEO TAPE	UNIT PRICE		QTY		AMOUNT
YOGA INSTRUCTIONS & PRACTICE SESSIONS	$39.95	X	_____	=	_____
ADVANCED YOGA SESSIONS LEVEL I	$29.95	X	_____	=	_____
ADVANCED YOGA SESSIONS LEVEL II	$29.95	X	_____	=	_____
YOGA FOR BUSY PEOPLE	$29.95	X	_____	=	_____
YOGA FOR YOUTHS	$29.95	X	_____	=	_____
YOGA FOR ACTIVE INDIVIDUALS	$29.95	X	_____	=	_____
YOGA FOR STRESS MANAGEMENT	$24.95	X	_____	=	_____
PRANAYAMA LEVEL I	$19.95	X	_____	=	_____
PRANAYAMA LEVEL II & MEDITATION	$24.95	X	_____	=	_____
YOGA FOR SENIORS	$24.95	X	_____	=	_____
YOGA FOR SENIORS WITH LUNG AILMENTS	$19.95	X	_____	=	_____
YOGA FOR THE EYES	$19.95	X	_____	=	_____
YOGA FOR PREGNANT WOMEN	$19.95	X	_____	=	_____
AUDIO TAPE **MEDITATION FOR ALL WALKS OF LIFE**	$ 6.95	X	_____	=	_____
COMPACT DISC **MEDITATION FOR ALL WALKS OF LIFE**	$12.95	X	_____	=	_____
PAPERBACK **THE POWER OF CONSCIOUS BREATHING IN HATHA YOGA**	$19.95	X	_____	=	_____

Sub Total _____

Shipping & Handling $4 per item _____

(Add $2 for every additional item) _____

California residents add 8.25% Sales Tax _____

Total _____

For detailed information: *www.indolink.com/vasantha* • To order online: *www.vasanthi-yoga.com*

Make check payable to 'Vasanthi Bhat' and mail to: VASANTHA YOGA 1196 Lynbrook Way, San Jose CA 95129
For information, call 408.257.8418 or e-mail: vasanthib@aol.com